Roald Dahl

WHO
WROTE
THAT?

Roald Dahl

Charles J. Shields

Chelsea House Publishers
Philadelphia

CHELSEA HOUSE PUBLISHERS

EDITOR IN CHIEF Sally Cheney
DIRECTOR OF PRODUCTION Kim Shinners
CREATIVE MANAGER Takeshi Takahashi
MANUFACTURING MANAGER Diann Grasse

STAFF FOR ROALD DAHL

ASSOCIATE EDITOR Benjamin Kim
PICTURE RESEARCHER Jane Sanders
PRODUCTION ASSISTANT Jaimie Winkler
COVER AND SERIES DESIGNER Keith Trego
LAYOUT 21st Century Publishing and Communications, Inc.

©2002 by Chelsea House Publishers,
a subsidiary of Haights Cross Communications.
All rights reserved. Printed and bound in the United States of America.

http://www.chelseahouse.com

3 5 7 9 8 6 4 2

Library of Congress Cataloging-in-Publication Data

Shields, Charles J., 1951–
   Roald Dahl / by Charles J. Shields.
      p. cm. — (Who wrote that?)
Summary: A description of the personal life and career of the twentieth-century
English writer of such successful books as "Charlie and the Chocolate Factory,"
"James and the Giant Peach," and "Matilda."
Includes bibliographical references and index.
   ISBN 0-7910-6722-X
   1. Dahl, Roald—Juvenile literature. 2. Authors, English—20th century—
Biography—Juvenile literature. 3. Children's stories—Authorship—Juvenile
literature. [1. Dahl, Roald. 2. Authors, English.] I. Title. II. Series.
PR6054.A35 Z875 2002
823'.914—dc21
                                                        2002000048

Table of Contents

A Gloster Gladiator plane like the one Roald Dahl flew and crashed into the desert. The biplane was still used in World War II by the British Royal Air Force even though it was no longer modern. This particular misadventure followed him throughout his life in different ways—in the form of a successful short story and also in a chronic back injury.

1

The Fighter Pilot Who Could Write

"I'm bowled over. Your piece is marvelous. It is the work of a gifted writer. I didn't touch a word of it."

—best-selling British author C.S. Forester
responding to Roald Dahl's first story

ON SEPTEMBER 19, 1940, high over a vast stretch of the Libyan desert, a British biplane buzzed against the blue sky like a lone dragonfly.

At the controls was a young man named Roald (roo-al) Dahl. He was 24 years old and 6' 6" tall—unusually tall for a pilot in the Royal Air Force (RAF). But with World War II breaking out the year before, Britain needed volunteers to face the enemy—the Germans in Europe, and the Italians in Africa. Dahl had been accepted immediately.

He had come to East Africa as a salesman for Shell Oil Company. Much to his mother's disappointment, he had refused to go to college at 18. "No, thank you," he had said to his mother. "I want to go straight from school to work for a company that will send me to wonderful faraway places like Africa or China."

And that's what had happened. He enjoyed his work in Dar-es-Salaam, the capital of Tanganyika (now Tanzania). He shuttled back and forth between gold mines, diamond mines, seaports, and oil fields. Sometimes, the temperature spiked above 105 degrees. He caught malaria, which is very unpleasant to have in a hot climate—one minute you're roasting with a high fever, and then suddenly you're shivering from chills. Nevertheless, the life in exotic faraway lands suited him, and he even learned to speak a little Swahili.

When Dahl reported for RAF duty in Nairobi, Kenya, a doctor examining him expressed doubts about his height. How could man as tall as he was squeeze into a cockpit designed for someone half a foot shorter? But the problem was overlooked and Dahl was enrolled in Initial Training School for pilots. There were 15 other young men like him, most of them former employees of large British-owned businesses in Africa, too. Of the 16, only three survived the war. But Dahl suspected nothing so foreboding at the time, as the whole routine of learning to fly seemed so carefree. "There was only one runway on the little Nairobi aerodrome," he wrote in *Going Solo*, a book about his RAF experiences, "and this gave everyone plenty of practice at crosswind landings and take-offs. And on most mornings, before flying began, we all had to run out on the airfield and chase the zebra away."

The planes they trained on were Tiger Moths—tough little machines that responded well to inexperienced pilots. "You could throw a Tiger Moth about all over the sky," remembered Dahl, "and nothing ever broke . . . You could spin her vertically downwards for thousands of feet and then all she needed was a touch on the rudder-bar, a bit of throttle and the stick pushed forward and out she came in a couple of flips." After going up a few times alone, he was allowed to cruise over the African plains at will. From elevations of only 60 or 70 feet, he would zoom over herds of buffalo and wildebeests, sending them stampeding in all directions. He flew over flocks of pink flamingoes in Lake Nakuru and around the summit of snow-capped Mount Kenya. "What a fortunate fellow I am, I kept telling myself," he wrote. "Nobody has ever had such a lovely time as this!"

After eight weeks, the "lovely" training came to an end. Dahl and his fellow airmen were sent to the big RAF base at Habbaniya in Iraq. Suddenly, "everything became suddenly much more serious," Dahl noted. Now they were flying Hawker Hart fighters powered by Rolls-Royce engines with machine guns mounted on the wings. They spent practically every morning from dawn to 11 a.m. pursuing targets. Around noon, the temperature reached 115 degrees and they rested. After six months, Dahl received his wings as a fighter pilot.

His next stop was an RAF base near the Suez Canal in Ismailia, Egypt, where he received his orders to join the 80th Squadron in Western Libya. Against the Italians, the

Hurricane fighter jets flying in formation. Dahl flew these over Greece and actually shot down German planes while serving in the 80th Squadron.

80th was flying Gloster Gladiators, which were old-fashioned biplane with twin machine guns that fired through the rotating propeller. Dahl marveled at how the guns worked, but there was no denying the plane was an outdated model that belonged in World War I, more than 20 years earlier. All the best fighters—the Spitfires and

Hurricanes—were being saved for the war in Europe.

After having received practically no instruction on the Gladiator, Dahl took off from Abu Suweir on September 19, 1940 to join the 80th Squadron in the desert. For hours, he droned monotonously through the sky alone. There was no radio on board, and the landscape far below was practically featureless. He set down twice to refuel, both times to get directions, but the 80th was on the move pursuing the Italians. He may have been given the wrong map coordinates.

As dusk began to fall and there was no sign of his destination, Dahl realized he was in a bad spot. He was lost and running out of fuel. There was only on thing to do—try to land the plane without the aid of an airstrip and before darkness fell. He pointed the plane earthward and hoped for the best.

The desert heaved up underneath his wheels unexpectedly fast. At 75 miles per hour, he clipped a boulder, sending the nose of the plane plowing into the sand like a missile. His face stuck the gun-sight, smashing his nose

Did you know...

Dahl's injuries from his plane crash required a hip replacement and two spinal operations, the last in 1947. Surgeons removed the fist-shaped end of his femur bone near his hip. Dahl always had a taste for grisly things, which certainly comes through in his writing. He kept the femur bone beside him in the backyard hut where he wrote everyday and used it as a paperweight.

and fracturing his skull. Flames spewed from the gas tanks. Wiping the blood off his face and trying to see, Dahl struggled painfully out of the cockpit, his hip and back badly injured by the impact. He tumbled out on the ground, and crawled away from the wreck. "My face hurt most," he recalled. "I slowly put a hand up to feel it. It was very sticky. My nose didn't seem to be there. I tried to feel my teeth to see if they were still there, but it seemed as though one or two were missing. And then the machine guns started off." Bullets from the heat-ignited ammunition slammed into stones and the sand around him, but Dahl lay still, as he was too injured to move. Hours later, a British army patrol found him and got him to safety.

He spent the next six months healing in various military hospitals, at the end of which he finally reported to the 80th squadron in early April 1941. By now, the outfit had been relocated to Greece and equipped with 18 Hurricane fighters—a pathetically small number compared to the strength of the German Luftwaffe, which was rumored to have 1,000 aircraft at its disposal.

Luck was with Dahl the first time he flew in combat, however. Pursuing six German Ju 88 bombers streaking for the safety of mountains, Dahl closed in on the last bomber in line, dodging fire from its tail-gunner. He squeezed the machine gun trigger. "The Hurricane gave a small shudder as the eight Brownings in the wings opened up together, and a second later I saw a huge piece of his metal engine-cowling the size of a dinner-tray go flying up into the air." The bomber rolled over, "turning slowly over and over like a leaf, the black smoke pouring out from the starboard engine. Then I saw one . . . two . . . three people jump out . . . I watched spellbound.

I couldn't believe that I had actually shot down a German bomber. But I was immensely relieved to see the parachutes." The next day, he sent a second bomber crashing into the Khalkis Bay near Athens before it could attack a Greek ship brimming with ammunition to be used against the Germans.

The Hurricanes flew a dozen raids, or "sorties" as they're called, during four days in mid-April. The Hurricanes were usually outnumbered in the air 10 to 1. On the fourth day, the squadron—now down to 12 planes—flew in tight formation over Athens to bait the Germans and give the Greeks hope. From the ground, 200 German Messerschmitt fighters rose up like flies to meet them. "Over Athens on that morning," Dahl recalled, "I can remember seeing our tight little formation all peeling away and disappearing among the swarms of enemy aircraft, and from then on, wherever I looked I saw an endless blur of enemy fighters whizzing towards me from every side. They came from above and they came from behind and they made frontal attacks from dead ahead, and I threw my Hurricane around as best I could and whenever a Hun [a German] came into my sights, I pressed the button."

Dahl fought until his guns were empty, weaving hard to avoid collisions, then returned to the base, his plane riddled with holes. Preparing to give his report in the Operations Room, he found his hands were shaking so badly he couldn't light a cigarette. "I looked at the other pilots. They were all holding cigarettes and their hands were all shaking as much as mine were. But I was feeling pretty good. I had stayed up there for thirty minutes and they hadn't got me. They got five of our twelve Hurricanes in that battle." Later that day, German fighters located the base and strafed it but didn't manage to destroy the seven remaining Hurricanes parked on the ground.

Dahl and the other men in 80th Squadron fought on despite the odds and despite discouraging news of a string of important German victories in Europe. But then Dahl's earlier injuries from the crash in the Libyan desert grew worse under the stress of flying. He suffered from blinding headaches and blacking out at the controls was only a matter of time. In June 1941, he was shipped home to England for medical reasons.

In London, Dahl had time to follow one of his passions, art collecting, and to meet a number of influential people. He was usually well-liked wherever he went, though some thought him too blunt and too fond of making wisecracks. In any case, his superiors decided that he could be put to use in Washington, D.C. building support for the Allies. The United States had declared war in December 1942, and pleasant young men like Dahl would make a good example of who had been doing the fighting on the British side since 1940. In January 1942, he arrived in Washington as an assistant air attaché for the British Embassy.

No sooner had he arrived than Dahl met another Briton who was also trying to do his part for the war, only as a writer instead. His name was C.S. Forester, author of a series of bestselling novels about the British navy in the early 19th century. Forester's readers followed the career of Horatio Hornblower, a teenage midshipman who, through bravery and good sense, rises over the years to admiral and commander-in-chief of the fleet. Forester had a contract with the *Saturday Evening Post*, one of the most popular magazines in the United States, to write articles about the current war. Hearing that a young RAF

C. S. Forester, a British author living in America who was so impressed by Dahl's writing that he sent one of Dahl's stories directly to the Saturday Evening Post.

pilot with combat experience was at the British Embassy, Forester paid him a visit, probably hoping to uncover a modern Horatio Hornblower.

Forester invited Dahl to lunch for an interview. As it turned out, Forester couldn't eat and take notes at the same time. Dahl gallantly volunteered to provide him with written descriptions of his experiences instead. What Forester received, however, was a full-fledged story, typed up by the embassy secretary. Dahl had titled it "A Piece of Cake." Forester was astonished by superior quality of the writing. He told Dahl he was gifted and had hardly changed a word. The editors at the *Saturday Evening Post*, however, were eager to add more dash and romance to the tale and changed the title to "Shot Down over Libya," which Dahl never had been. In addition, they illustrated the article with a picture of a Hurricane, instead of the clumsy Gladiator biplane that Dahl had crashed in the desert. Ten days after Forester submitted the piece, Dahl received a check for

Did you know...

In "Shot Down Over Libya," Dahl made sure the reader understood that flying a fighter plane in the desert was not as glamorous as it appeared:

"It was getting hot in the cockpit. My shirt and pants were dark with sweat, and I smelt like hell. You can't take a bath in four pints of water a day when you've got to use it for drinking as well; at least I can't, because I'm pretty big. Wonder if Shorty could. But then he smelled, too, and so did the C.O. [Commanding Officer] Jimmy smelt worst of all. He used to come into breakfast every morning and say, 'Hell, I smell good today,' and nobody took any notice."

$1,000 and a request from the *Post* for more stories. "Shot Down Over Libya" appeared in the magazine in August 1942.

The young salesman-turned-pilot—who would eventually write 19 children's books, nine collections of short stories, and numerous screenplays and television scripts—had taken a first and unexpected step toward becoming a writer. It would be years, however, before he tapped into the richest source of his creativity for stories—his own childhood. Those stories would make him one of the most popular authors in the world.

Dahl at age 3 with his mother Mormor. Dahl's life was already unusual from the start, as he was born of Norwegian parents and living in Wales. Soon he would face tragedies like the deaths of his sister and father. Thankfully, his mother Mormor was a strong woman who stayed strong in the face of adversity.

2

Boy

"I was appalled by the fact that masters and senior boys were allowed literally to wound other boys, and sometimes quite severely. I couldn't get over it. I never got over it."

—Roald Dahl

ROALD DAHL'S FATHER had one arm.

When Roald's father Harald was fourteen years old and living in his hometown of Sarpsborg, Norway, he was standing on a roof and helping to repair it when the tiles shifted and he fell. His parents, suspecting he had broken his arm, called a doctor.

The man arrived drunk. He insisted the boy's elbow was only dislocated and had to be wrenched back into place. Enlisting two other men to help, the doctor took hold of Harald's arm. "Pull men, pull! Pull as hard as you can!" the doctor ordered. The injured boy screamed and his mother shouted, "Stop!" But it was too late, and Harald's arm bone tore through the skin of his forearm.

"This was in 1877 and orthopaedic surgery was not what it is today," Dahl wrote in his is autobiographical *Boy: Tales of Childhood*. "So they simply amputated the arm at the elbow and for the rest my life my father had to manage with one arm."

The matter-of-fact way that Dahl describes this mishap reveals an important clue about him. In his own life, he would face a series of misfortunes, some of them terrible to imagine, but he would do his best to conquer the "enemy"—whether it was grief, physical disabilities, or illness. Many of Dahl's main characters in his children's books are the same way—they fight back in life. His father and mother set the example.

As a young man, Harald Dahl had big plans for going into business, but he realized that Norway was too poor. So he settled in Paris with his brother to make a start. The two eventually separated, agreeing it was best to be independent of each other. In Paris, Harald met and married a young woman named Marie. He went into partnership with another Norwegian named Aadnesen, and they set themselves up as shipbrokers, supplying everything a ship needs, such as ropes, paint, decking, and coal. But because coal was the most necessary and profitable item needed by steamships in those days, the firm of "Aadnesen and Dahl" relocated to Cardiff, Wales—one of the great coaling ports of the world.

A residential neighborhood in Cardiff, Wales. Dahl grew up in the village of Radyr near Cardiff, a coal port located in western England.

Marie bore two children in Cardiff, but she died giving birth to the second. In 1911, Harald returned to Norway, hoping to meet a young woman who might consider marrying a widower with two children. There he met, fell in love with, and proposed to Sofie Magdalene Hesselberg. In a photograph of her taken during her engagement, she is walking outside on a breezy day and smiling. Most people posed rather solemnly for pictures in those days, but Sophie gives an impression of energy. During the next six years, she bore four children—two girls (Astri, Alfhild) a boy (Roald), and then another girl (Else).

Roald was born September 13, 1916 in Llandaff, Wales.

By now, Harald Dahl was a wealthy businessman with a large family—six children in all—and he purchased a mansion in the village of Radyr near Cardiff. Despite the pressures of his business, he found time for hobbies. In *Boy*, Roald writes that his father was an admirer and collector of "lovely paintings and fine furniture." Roald would later become an art and wine collector himself. The elder Dahl was also a first-rate gardener who liked alpine plants, probably because they reminded him of Norway. His son developed a passion for gardening, too, especially raising orchids.

Perhaps most important to Roald the future writer was the fact that his father was a disciplined diary-keeper. "I still have one of his many notebooks from the Great War of 1914-18," he wrote in *Boy*. "Every single day during those five war years he would write several pages of comment and observation about the events of the time." When he was eight, Roald kept his own secret diary, too. "To make sure that none of my sisters got hold of it and read it, I used to put it in a waterproof tin box tied to a branch at the very top of an enormous conker tree in our garden. I knew they couldn't climb up there. Then every day I would go up myself and get it out and sit in the tree and make the entries for the day."

Sophie, called Mormor by her family, participated in her husband's interests in addition to being a devoted parent. Remembering his mother in *Memories With Food*, Roald recalled that "she had a crystal-clear intellect and a deep interest in almost everything . . . her children radiated around her like planets round a sun." When Sophie was pregnant with a fifth child, Asta, however, the family was struck by a sudden double loss. In 1920, the eldest daughter, Astri, age 7, died of appendicitis. The blow literally killed Dahl's father. "Astri was far and away my father's favorite," Roald wrote in *Boy*. "He adored her beyond measure and her sudden death left him literally speechless for day afterwards. He was so overwhelmed with grief that when he himself went down with pneumonia a month or so afterwards . . . . [he] refused to fight. He was thinking, I am quite sure, of his beloved daughter, and he was wanting to join her in heaven." Harald Dahl died soon after at age 57.

Although Dahl describes what Astri's death meant to his father and what his father's death in turn meant to his mother, he is silent about how his father's death affected him, who was at the time only four years old. Some his biographers have suggested Dahl would have believed his father wanted to be with his daughter more than he wanted to continue living to be with his son. Unfortunate too was the fact that Mormor, although an excellent mother, was not physically affectionate, which would have helped soothe Roald's sorrow. When Dahl's first wife Patricia Neal met Mormor and the rest of the family for the first time, she noted in her autobiography *As I Am* that "There was no kiss. No embrace. In fact, as welcome as they made me feel, not one of them greeted me with a kiss that day." Jeremy Treglown, the author of the most thorough biography of Dahl, wrote that Dahl was a lonely child. Many of Dahl's child characters are orphans or only children, perhaps as a reflection of the way Dahl felt.

Nevertheless, Mormor—with four surviving children of her own and two step-children—showed remarkable strength when her family needed her. Dahl wrote that a "less courageous woman" would've simply taken them all to Norway. But Harald had made it clear he wanted his children educated in English schools because they were superior, and Mormor was determined to carry out her late husband's wishes. First she moved the family into a smaller, more manageable home in Llandaff, and then she sent each of the children one by one to a local school called Elmtree House for kindergarten.

When Roald turned seven, he was enrolled at Llandaff Cathedral School, a private boy's school. He didn't like it, or any schooling for that matter. Many of his fictional characters feel the same way. As a little boy, he had been free to roam the Dahl estate under the adoring eyes of his parents. But school, he later wrote, was made up of "days of horrors, of fierce discipline, of not talking in the dormitories, no running in the corridors, no untidiness of any sort, no this or that or the other, just rules, rules and still more rules that had to be obeyed." Home life was much more to his liking, mainly because Sophie made it so comfortable.

As Roald grew from a small boy to a teenager, the Dahl home became a kind of refuge. Roald's family nickname was "the apple" because he was the apple of his mother's eye. At home, the Dahls spoke their own language around each other— a mixture of Norwegian and English. Mormor read the children tales about trolls and other mythical Norwegian creatures. "She was a great teller of tales," Dahl recalled. "Her memory was prodigious and nothing that ever happened to her in her life was forgotten." During the summers, she took them all to Norway to visit relatives. In his book *The Witches*, Dahl's Norwegian heritage comes out strongly, and he bases the character of the grandmother admiringly on his mother.

In fact, in some ways, the Dahls remained apart from Welsh and English society, which may explain why Dahl's

Dahl in a school uniform. School proved to be an unpleasant place for young Roald, and he was forever angry at the way the older kids and headmasters would beat the younger boys. This hatred for authoritarian abuse would show up many times in his books.

characters are often outsiders, too. Mormor's foreignness was even flung in her face as an insult when Roald got into trouble once at Llandaff Cathedral School. The incident stemmed from a prank over candy.

Roald had a sweet tooth, a craving he celebrated in *Charlie and the Chocolate Factory*. On the way home from school, he and his friends would stop by a shop that sold sweets. But entering it was like going into a dragon's cave—only the dragon was the owner, Mrs. Pratchett. "She was a small skinny old hag with a moustache on her upper lip and a mouth as sour as a green gooseberry. She never smiled. She never welcomed us when we went in, and the only times she spoke were when she said things like, 'I'm watchin' you so keep yer thievin' fingers off them chocolates!' or 'I don't want you in 'ere just to look around! Either you *forks* out or you *gets* out!'"

Dahl and his friends decided to get revenge on Mrs. Pratchett by slipping a dead mouse into the Gobstoppers jar when her back was turned. She was not so easily tricked, however, and charged over to the school nearly hysterical with rage. She identified the culprits, and Dahl and the others were summoned to the headmaster's study, where they were each giving a caning—swatted with a cane on their rear ends while they bent over. Mrs. Prachett witnessed the beatings gleefully from a chair in the corner. "At first I heard only the *crack* and felt absolutely nothing at all," Dahl wrote in *Boy*, "but a fraction of a second later the burning sting that flooded across my buttocks was so terrific that all I could do was gasp."

That night, while Roald was getting ready for his bath, Mormor noticed his red welts. He explained what had happened and she went immediately to see the headmaster. When she returned, Roald asked he what the headmaster had said. "He told me I was a foreigner and didn't under-stand how British schools were run," was her reply. As she disapproved of physical punishment, Mormor removed her son from the school.

At the age of nine, he was placed in St. Peter's Preparatory School in Weston-Super-Mare, a boarding school where he would live during the school year until he was 13. At first, he was so homesick he faked appendicitis. He wrote his mother every week, which became a habit that continued until the end of World War II. He signed every letter "Boy." When Mormor died in 1967, Dahl was astonished to discover that she had kept every one of his letters written between 1925-1945. (Later, when his own children went to boarding school, Roald wrote to them twice a week to brighten up the drudgery of their school days.)

Dahl got along fairly well at boarding school. Schoolmates remembered him as a tall, soft-faced boy, not especially popular but very close to the few boys who became his friends. He was good at sports like cricket and swimming, but academically he was toward the bottom of his class. He liked to read, and some of his favorite novelists were the adventure writers Rudyard Kipling, Captain Marryat, H. Rider Haggard, and G.A. Henty. Their books, emphasizing heroism and masculinity, were a good fit with his own values, which emerged in his own writing, especially in stories for adults.

But just like in his childrens' books, Dahl's world was again populated with harsh, unfeeling adults like Mrs. Pratchett, the candy store owner, and the headmaster at Llandaff who had caned him. This time the object of his scorn—and even hatred—was St. Peter's headmistress. No doubt Dahl had this woman or someone like her in mind when he wrote his bitter portrait of Miss Trunchbull in *Matilda*. Dahl once remarked that what made him different from most other children's writers was "this business of remembering what it was like to be young." His portrait of Miss Trunchbull confirms that. She is described from the point of view of child as if she were a brutal fairytale giant:

> She was above all a most formidable female. She had once been a famous athlete, and even now the muscles were still clearly in evidence. You could see them in the bull-neck, in the big shoulders, in the thick arms, in the sinewy wrists and in the powerful legs. Looking at her, you got the feeling that this was someone who could bend iron bars and tear telephone directories in half. Her face, I'm afraid, was neither a thing of beauty nor a joy forever. She had an obstinate chin, a cruel mouth and small arrogant eyes. And as for her clothes . . . they were, to say the least, extremely odd. She always had on a brown cotton smock, which was pinched in around the waist with a wide leather belt. The belt was fastened in front with an enormous silver buckle. The massive thighs which emerged from out of the smock were encased in a pair of extraordinary breeches, bottle-green in colour and made of coarse twill. The breeches reached to just below the knees and from there on down she sported greet stockings with turn-up tops, which displayed her calf muscles to perfection. On her feet she wore flat–heeled brown brogues with leather flaps. She looked, in short, more like a rather eccentric and blood-thirsty follower of the stag-hounds than the headmistress of a nice school for children.

By the time Roald was 13, the family had moved from Cardiff to Kent and he was sent next to Repton Public School in Derbyshire. (In England, a "public" school is a private school.) The family had to sell off jewelry to pay for his tuition and upkeep. But to Roald, Repton was even worse than St. Peter's. Younger boys called "fags" were expected to be the personal servants of older boys known as "boazers." Boazers were permitted to cane the younger

Dahl on a trip to Newfoundland. After high school, he found the idea of college to be far less exciting than visiting faraway lands.

boys and they did so, priding themselves on how fast and accurately they could leave bleeding stripes on bare skin. This kind of tradition angered Roald and he never forgot it. On Sundays, he got revenge of a sort by walking three miles to a nearby village where he kept a motorcycle in a rented garage. Donning a helmet, goggles, and wind jacket, he would roar through the middle of Repton village on his motorcycle, sailing past scowling teachers out for a quiet Sunday stroll. Once, he remembered, "I found myself motoring within a couple of yards of the terrifying figure of the headmaster, Dr. Geoffrey Fisher himself, as he strode with purposeful step towards the chapel. He glared at me as I rode past, but I don't think that it would have entered his brainy head for one moment that I was a member of the school."

Academically, Roald continued to bump along the bottom of his class. His English teacher judged him to be "quite incapable of marshalling his thoughts on paper"—a fascinating comment in retrospect about the future writer.

Did you know...

Dahl remained bitter his entire life about the beatings at Repton. In *Boy: Tales of Childhood* he alleges that faculty member Geoffrey Fisher was deliberately sadistic. The fact that Fisher could have delivered vicious beatings and then gone on to become Archbishop of Canterbury (the highest office in the Anglican Church in Britain) and then crowned by Queen Elizabeth II in Westminster Abbey, Dahl argued, made him doubt the existence of God. In his biography of Dahl, however, Jeremy Treglown discovers that Dahl misremembered. The beatings he was referring to happened in 1933, a year after Fisher left Repton. Dahl must have mixed up Fisher with J. T. Christie, his successor.

One of the only bright lights at Repton was the Cadbury chocolate factory located not far away. The boys were given boxes of free chocolate to sample in return for their feedback on the candy. Dahl dreamed of working in the inventing room of a chocolate factory, and in *Charlie and the Chocolate Factory*, he described such a place straight out of his fantasies.

By the time he was ready to graduate from Repton at 18 and begin the next phrase of his education by attending a university, Roald decided he'd had enough of schooling. He turned down his mother's offer to pay for his education and took a sales position with Shell Oil Company instead, and he was off to East Africa. World events interrupted his plans, however, and the salesman became a fighter pilot whose experiences later would serve him well as a beginning writer.

The Saturday Evening Post, *which published Dahl's first short story about his crash in the desert, ultimately launching his writing career.*

3

"I Began to See I Could Handle Fiction"

" . . . he saw a little man, scarcely more than six inches high, with a large round face and a little pair of horns growing out of his head. On his legs were a pair of shiny black suction boots, which made it possible for him to remain standing on the wing at 300 miles an hour."

—from Roald Dahl's first children's book,
The Gremlins (1943)

AFTER THE PUBLICATION of "Shot Down Over Libya" in August 1942, the *Saturday Evening Post* asked for more stories. And as the British air attaché in Washington, it was partly Dahl's job to be a conversationalist and to tell stories. At dinners around Washington—and he was invited to many—Dahl had a reputation for the stories he'd tell about his adventures in as an RAF fighter pilot. Experimenting with off-the-cuff stories on listeners was a favorite technique of his. Later in life when he wrote children's books regularly, Dahl would try out plots on his own children first. "Roald had a foolproof system for developing his tales," remembered his first wife, Patricia Neal. "He would tell them to the children and if they asked to hear one again, he knew he had a winner."

On the Washington dinner circuit, a dependable yarn that always amused listeners at the table was the one about gremlins. According to him, gremlins were like mischievous elves, except that their specialty was ruining mechanical things. In the RAF, Dahl explained tongue-in-cheek, gremlins were constantly pulling out wires in control panels, drilling holes in wings that looked like bullet holes, and generally making machines go mad. What did they look like? Well, they dressed sort of like aviators themselves, only they were very small and devilish.

Then Dahl would add some supposedly actual cases involving gremlins that made his story all the more fun. He later claimed that he invented gremlins, although RAF pilots had been kidding about them for years. In any case, the story went over so well that Dahl decided to write it up. He called it "Gremlin Lore." But first he had to submit it to the British Information Services for approval, which was the rule regarding public statements from the embassy.

Sidney Bernstein, the information officer who read it, happened to be a good friend of Walt Disney's. The Walt Disney Company was not the entertainment giant then that it is now. Four full-length Disney films in a row—*Pinocchio, Fantasia, Dumbo*, and *Bambi*—had all been received mildly by audiences distracted by war news, and the studio was eager to find entertaining, war-related features. When Bernstein shared "Gremlin Lore" with Walt Disney in July 1942, Disney snapped it up as an ideal short subject. Dahl was invited to Hollywood to help with the screenplay. Disney placed the story "The Gremlins" with *Cosmopolitan* magazine, in which it appeared in December. Dahl used a pen name "Pegasus" after the winged horse from mythology.

Did you know...

Copies of Dahl's first book for children, *The Gremlins*, are rare today, valued at about $1,000 each. The book went out of print after the first edition during World War II, and Dahl chose not to renew the copyright after he became a well-known author. When Disney decided not to make an animated movie based on the book, Warner Brothers borrowed the gremlins idea instead. In the cartoon "Falling Hare" (1943), Bugs Bunny hysterically tries to fight off a gremlin that sabotages his bomber in flight.

Unfortunately, creative issues cropped up right away after Dahl arrived in Hollywood. What did gremlins look like exactly? Where did they live, and why did they destroy machines—just for the sheer delight of wrecking them? Leprechauns play tricks because they're protecting a pot of gold, but what's the motive of a gremlin? It wasn't even clear if the subject should be light-hearted or serious. After all, pilots were killed by their airplane's mechanical failures. Moreover, Walt Disney doubted the studio could copyright a word already in common use. Disney was known to work by instinct, and following a hunch, he backed finally away from "The Gremlins" altogether and stopped production.

For Dahl, the nosedive of the whole project was not a total loss. Random House published *The Gremlins: A Royal Air Force Story by Flight Lieutenant Roald Dahl* as a picture book for children in 1943. The young writer's first book was out and it received good reviews. The *New York Times* Book Review praised the author for his "adeptness in building up a tall tale in the American tradition." The *Weekly Book Review* said that other stories about gremlins seemed ridiculous, but as a fantasy, Dahl's "book is different. It is the Real Thing."

In later years, however, Dahl did not like *The Gremlins* being referred to as his first children's book. Anyone who reads it online today will immediately notice that the tone is amateurish. The narrator is clearly an adult talking down to small children about things they don't care about—planes, war, men joking with each other, and so on. All his writing life, Dahl couldn't resist peeping out from behind his mask as narrator and trying to also amuse the adults reading his books to their

Walt Disney at work in 1942. His studio was looking to make war-related pictures and he was very interested in Dahl's children's story The Gremlins, *based on war stories British pilots told which blamed imaginary creatures on their aircraft's mechincal problems. Unfortunately talks ultimately broke down and Disney did not produce the film.*

children. *The Gremlins* is his worst example of that tendency, and perhaps Dahl realized it. He chose not to renew the copyright.

Nevertheless, these early successes encouraged him, and by the fall of 1944 Dahl had an agent marketing his stories. "The Sword" appeared in *The Atlantic Monthly*; "Katina" and "Only This" in the *Ladies' Home Journal*; and "Beware of the Dog" in *Harper's*. Each one contained a heavy dose of war propaganda, but "Katina" comes close to being a reassuring tale for children. When a German bombing raid kills the parents of a Greek girl, pilots from an RAF squadron find her, attend to her injuries, and take care of her. Much later, orphans figure as main characters in *James and the Giant Peach*, *The BFG*, and *The Twits*.

By the war's end in 1945, Dahl had racked up a remarkable string of sales for a new writer—16 stories in magazines and not a single rejection. His stories, he said, "became less and less realistic and more fictional. I began to see I could handle fiction." With the income from writing, he built up his art collection—Matisses, enormous Fauve Roualts, Soutines, Cézanne watercolors, Bonnards, Boudins, a Renoir, a Sisley, a Degas landscape. "I have very good pictures," he boasted later, "which I bought because I loved them and usually they were cheap, a long time ago."

That year, 1945, he returned to England to the country village of Amersham to be near his mother, but with a definite career goal in mind. He was going to write full-time. Dahl enjoyed country life. It reminded him of his happiness living in the big rambling manor on an estate in Wales. He got down to work right away and put together a collection of ten war stories about flying. Some were drawn from personal experience, some adapted from events, and a few were completely original.

In 1946, *Over to You* appeared in the United States and Britain to mixed reviews. *The Saturday Review*, for example, praised Dahl for his "vivid imagination" and his ability to create "startling images," predicting that the author had real promise. Yet *Over to You* didn't sell very well, perhaps in part because readers were tired of lightweight fiction about the war. When novels about the war with real literary merit about the war came along, however, like Norman Mailer's *The Naked and the Dead*, or James Jones' *From Here to Eternity*, they became bestsellers.

Perhaps realizing this trend, Dahl decided to take an ambitious risk as an author and tackle a serious subject —nuclear war—in a satirical way. Dahl liked to brag that one of the most famous editors of the 20th century, Maxwell Perkins, who had worked with American author F. Scott Fitzgerald, heard his story idea and encouraged him to write it.

The novel *Sometime Never: A Tale of Supermen* appeared in the United States in 1948 published by Scribner's and a year later in Britain by Collins. Dahl starts out the book with gremlins living underground. They are debating a plan to come above ground and try to seize the world for themselves. But then the head gremlin realizes there's no need—people will destroy themselves. World War III indeed breaks out, killing millions. Not satisfied with the catastrophe caused by a third world war, the surviving global powers launch World War

IV. Humanity foolishly succeeds in exterminating itself. The gremlins emerge from below ground to rule the planet, but find it ruined for any living thing now.

The book flopped. *The Kirkus Review* said it was not as well written as the stories in *Over To You*. The *New York Times* reviewer thought that the book had some strong points but "they could have been said with less repetition, less preliminary build-up and fewer words." Dahl wrote off his attempt at a novel as a "practice session" and decided to stick to short stories instead. He may also have felt that by living in England, he was out of the post-war literary loop centered in New York. His stories were appearing in *Collier's* and the *New Yorker*, but he was not in America rubbing elbows with the kind

Did you know...

As a British air attaché posted to Washington, DC part of Dahl's job was to inspire goodwill between the United States and his home country. Publication of *The Gremlins* provided him with a extraordinarily lucky break. Eleanor Roosevelt, wife of the 32nd president of the United States, read the book to her grandchildren. Since he was stationed in Washington, Dahl received an invitation to visit the Roosevelts, and soon he was a regular dinnertime guest at the White House. No doubt British Prime Minister Winston Churchill gained some insights from Dahl's reports on the First Family.

of people he enjoyed—artists, fellow writers, socialites —and getting fresh ideas.

In 1950, he applied for and received an American visa. He moved to New York, and quickly rejoined the social round of dinners he enjoyed so much. It was at one of them in 1951 that he was introduced to a young actress making a name for herself on the stage and movie screen—Patricia Neal.

Roald Dahl and Patricia Neal in 1954. Neal was an established actress when she met Dahl, and found it infuriating when he ignored her throughout their first meeting at a large dinner party. Ultimately it turned out that Dahl merely feigned disinterest, as he asked her out a few days following the party. The two married in 1953.

4

Writing for Adults

"[His] stories are bizarre, inventive, clever, imaginative, spinechilling . . . For kindness and pleasantries, I suggest you look elsewhere."

—a book reviewer describing
Dahl's early horror stories

ONCE AGAIN, DAHL'S reputation as a clever dinner table conversationalist and storyteller made him a popular dinner guest in New York social circles. He loved to shock unprepared listeners with his wit and sarcasm. Perhaps that's why Lillian Hellman—a playwright with a tart tongue herself—

invited him to one of her dinner parties in 1951.

Five years earlier in 1946, Hellman's play *Another Part of the Forest*, about a troubled southern family in the 1880s, created the hottest-selling tickets on Broadway. One of the play's stars was Patricia Neal. Neal was a southerner herself, born in Packard, Kentucky. After attending Northwestern University, she left to pursue her career goal as an actress in New York. She had a kind of regal beauty coupled with a dark, smoky voice. She chose her roles carefully. Most called for characters who were smart, passionate, but tough-minded women like herself. Hellman encouraged the young actress' spunk and thought she would make a good match seated next to Dahl, the wise-acre.

Neal expected an evening of idle talk and flirting. But instead Dahl mostly ignored her, preferring to chat with another person at the table—symphony composer Leonard Bernstein. The rebuff surprised and intrigued her. She had only recently ended a painful love affair in Hollywood, which the tabloids had been gleefully reporting. Yet Dahl—distinguished, ten years older than she, and British—didn't seem to care who she was, or how notorious the gossip columnists said she was. She left the dinner that night "loathing Roald Dahl."

Several days later, she was surprised when he phoned her and asked for a date. He said he had gotten her number from their hostess, Lillian Hellman. She said no. He called again. This time she gave in, although guardedly. From then on he began picking her up after her theater rehearsals, still acting like he had nothing better to do. According to her autobiography, she didn't fall in love with him, but his determination impressed her. Also in his favor, although unknown to him at the time, Neal was looking forward to starting a family. In

Dahl, she saw a strong, take-charge person who might make a good partner in life.

One night after a performance, Pat went backstage to find him waiting for her. With typical nonchalance and little build-up, he said, "I would like to know how you think it would work if we got married." "Oh no!" she said. "Roald, let's just continue the way we are. I mean, let's not talk about that now. All right?" But less than a year later, they were married on July 2, 1953 at Trinity Church in New York. They honeymooned in the Mediterranean. Dahl insisted they rent a snazzy sportscar and drive around Europe, too.

1953 was an unforgettable year for the author all around. He was deep into his career of writing for adults and it was going extremely well. He was not a quick writer, sometimes spending six months on a story, "sometimes as much as a month on the first page," he said. And he refused to go ahead unless he had a good plot in mind. Nevertheless, his stories appeared regularly in the *New Yorker*, *Harpers*, and the *Atlantic Monthly*—all topflight magazines carrying leading authors.

Did you know...

Dahl never cared much what other people thought of him. Even as a young man, he had a strong and forceful personality. In her autobiography *As I Am*, Dahl's first wife, actress Patricia Neal, described the impression he made. She said he was an individualist, cultured and witty. He towered over most people at 6'6", and when Dahl boomed "Well done!" Neal said it was "as if God Himself were bestowing the credit."

GARY COOPER   PATRICIA NEAL

A PICTURE
TO REMEMBER
FROM
WARNER
BROS.

THE FOUNTAINHEAD

Patricia Neal and co-star Gary Cooper in a movie poster for their film The Fountainhead. *Neal was already an established actress by the time she met Dahl, and her career continued to prosper during their marriage.*

That year, book publisher Alfred A. Knopf brought out a collection of Dahl's stories titled *Someone Like You* with such favorites as "Taste," "My Lady Love, My Dove," "Skin," and "Dip in the Pool," all of which later ended up in short story anthologies. A series of four stories set in the English countryside about Claud and his dog become popular on their own. The character Claud was based on butcher Claud Taylor in Amersham whom Dahl had befriended.

The 18 stories in *Someone Like You* are filled with Dahl's love of macabre touches and bitter reversals. Many characters appear to be normal, but gradually it becomes clear they have a hidden, nasty side. A reviewer for the *Sunday Tribune* wrote, "[Dahl's] stories are bizarre, inventive, clever, imaginative, spinechilling . . . For kindness and pleasantries, I suggest you look elsewhere. If, on the other hand, it is dark ingenuity you're after with lashings of malice and a slice of humour then Roald Dahl is the man." A *New York Times* critic compared him with O. Henry and enthused, "At disconcertingly long intervals, the *compleat* short-story writer comes along . . . Tension is his business; give him a surprise denouement, he'll give you a story leading up to it. His name in this instance is Roald Dahl."

A reviewer for the *Saturday Review* put his finger on the key to Dahl's method. He said it was the contrast between the narrator's tone and what was happening in the story. Dahl pitted a "matter-of-fact and realistic method" of storytelling against "his surprise endings."

Later in his children's books, he managed the effect skillfully again. On the very first page of *James and the Giant Peach*, for instance, young readers learn that four-year-old James Henry Trotter had a very happy life. "Then, one day, James's mother and father went to London to do some shopping, and there a terrible thing happened. Both of them suddenly got eaten up (in full daylight, mind you, and on a crowded street) by an enormous, angry rhinoceros which had escaped from the London Zoo." The incident is ridiculous, but Dahl reports it as absolutely true and continues on matter-of-factly with what happened to James after that.

The success of *Someone Like You* brought Dahl his first

major literary prize, the Edgar Allen Poe award given to him by the prestigious Mystery Writers of America in 1954. He received it again in 1959 for other stories. The following year, Knopf published a second collection Dahl's tales, *Kiss, Kiss*. Pat had mentioned to Roald that she knew an actress who peppered her phone calls to her husband with "kiss, kiss" and Dahl took it for a title. The stories in *Someone Like You* and *Kiss, Kiss* became the basis for "Tales of the Unexpected," a hugely popular British television program in the 1960s hosted by Dahl and starring famous actors such as John Gielgud, Alec Guinness and Joan Collins.

Did you know...

Patricia Neal was already famous as an actress when Roald Dahl met her. She had won a Tony in 1946—the equivalent of an Academy Award for stage-acting—at the age of 20 for her role Lillian Hellman's play *Another Part Of The Forest*. *Life* magazine— the most popular magazine of the day— featured her on its cover. Neal then made several movies, the first being *The Hasty Heart* with future president Ronald Reagan. Real stardom came in 1949 for her role in *The Fountainhead*, based on Ayn Rand's best-selling novel and co-starring one of the biggest romantic leads in Hollywood at the time, Gary Cooper. In 1953, Neal and Dahl were married. Ten years later, Neal won an Academy Award for *Hud* (1963) with Paul Newman.

In the meantime, the Dahls had started a family. Daughters Oliva and Tessa had been born in 1955 and 1957 respectively. Dahl fell into the pleasant habit of telling them stories at bedtime, one of which was about a lonely boy who discovered a giant peach in his backyard. And in 1960 Pat gave birth to a son, Theo.

Then one afternoon that year, four-month-old Theo was out for a ride in his baby carriage with a nanny in the busy Manhattan section of New York City. They paused at the street corner and waited for the light to change. When it did, they proceeded across the intersection. A speeding cab ran the stoplight, stuck the baby carriage, and hurled it into the side of a bus.

It was the first of several major emotional challenges that Dahl would confront in the coming decade. In characteristic style, he regarded each one like an enemy to be overcome. Self-pity was not in his nature and did not tolerate it in other people, either. Following the sudden deaths of his sister and father during his childhood, he had carried on with no special molly-coddling then. Nor had he complained about his war injuries and surgical operations to his hip and back.

What had happened to his son, and was yet to happen to other family members, he would not accept without a fight.

Roald, Pat and children Theo, Ophelia and Tessa in Great Missenden. Despite the tragedies of Theo's accident, daughter Olivia's death and wife Pat's series of strokes, Dahl refused to sit idly by and wallow in misery. This matter-of-fact attitude about overcoming obstacles can be seen in his own books, especially the tone in which certain catastrophes are described.

5

The Challenges of Life

"It cannot be said that the series of misfortunes and tragedies Dahl was to suffer made him more bitter. Loss and physical adversity seemed to stimulate his enormous energies to positive action. He fought misfortune as if it was a dragon to be slain."

—Peter Lennon,
The (Manchester, UK) *Guardian* newspaper, 1996

THE DOUBLE IMPACT of Theo first being struck by a car and then thrown against a bus caused severe head injuries. He was temporarily blinded. Swelling caused by fluid inside his head created hydrocephalus, commonly known as "water on the brain." He would need months of hospital care and therapy, doctors informed his parents. Even so, there was a chance that their infant son would suffer permanent neurological damage.

At the time of the accident, Roald was just beginning a new phase in his career as a writer. He had turned the bedtime story for his daughters about the boy and the giant peach into the manuscript *James and the Giant Peach*. It would be out two years later in 1962. Writing a children's book was such an enjoyable change from penning adult stories that Dahl had begun a second story. It would involve one of his childhood loves—chocolate. The working title was "Charlie's Chocolate Boy." But now with his infant son critically injured, he put all that aside and turned his energies—and his imagination, too—on remedying the catastrophe that had struck his family.

First, he attacked the problem of Theo remaining hospitalized. According to the doctors, the constant life-threatening issue was fluid build-up on the brain. It had to be monitored and the fluid drained using a machine-assisted shunt that often clogged, unfortunately. But once Roald had a grasp of the problem, he researched it thoroughly, and went into action. Enlisting the help of two friends—airplane engine engineer Stanley Wade and neurosurgeon Kenneth Till—he explained their goal: to create a dependable, pressure-sensitive value that could be implanted in a brain-injured person. It would respond automatically to fluid build-up, and drain it using the body's own internal systems. A machine by the bedside would be unnecessary.

Working as a team, the three men spent months design-ing and testing models. As it turned out, Theo recovered enough not to need the Dahl-Wade-Till valve when it was ready in June 1962. Over the years, however, hospitals used 2,000-3,000 of the values to assist head-injury victims until new technological developments surpassed its usefulness.

With Theo's recovery as well in hand as could be expected, Dahl addressed what he saw as the next problem, which was assuring his family's safety.

In 1960, not long after Theo could safely make the trip, the Dahl family sold their apartment in Manhattan. They moved to a house in Buckinghamshire, England located in the village of Great Missenden, only eight miles from Roald's mother in Amersham. For the next 20 years, Roald and Pat would divide their time between England

Did you know...

Tessa Dahl recalls that the pain of her brother's accident and the death of her sister cast a pall at times over her family, but she still counts herself fortunate for other reasons. "When I was a teenager I had a pretty rocky time, but that was nobody's fault. A horrible succession of tragedies rather deprived me of a full chance to indulge my adolescence. Yet I had been given a wonderful launching pad. Brought up as the first child to hear *James and the Giant Peach, Charlie and the Chocolate Factory, The Magic Finger* and *Fantastic Mr. Fox,* I was immunized against the predictable."

and the United States while the children grew up in the English countryside.

The name Missenden is thought to come from the old English words *mysse* and *denu*, meaning "valley where water-plants or marsh-plants grow." Great Missenden is at the head of the Misbourne valley, a small village with a long curving High Street of half-timbered and centuries-old shops and pubs. In the mid-19th century, Robert Louis Stevenson, the author of *Treasure Island*, had found it to be a good place to write.

The Dahls purchased a Georgian-style home on a quiet lane and named it Gypsy House. To add to their new home's free-spirited feeling, Roald hired a carpenter friend to build him a gypsy wagon at the bottom of the garden. Inside this hut, writing day after day, he would make his reputation as one of the most famous children's authors in the world. But not long after they

Did you know...

Despite his flinty, difficult side, Dahl was generous with his time and money in helping other people. In the 1960s, for example, he arranged for a busload of children from a Southern Italian orphanage to vacation in the village of Great Missenden where he lived. Over the years, he received many requests for help. Having suffered through his daughter Olivia's early death and his son Theo's long rehabilitation, Dahl frequently assisted families with seriously ill or disabled children.

were settled in Great Missenden, misfortune arrived there, too.

In the 1960s, measles was considered one of several routine childhood diseases, including chicken pox and the mumps. Measles inoculation was on the rise in the United States but was almost unknown in England. In mid-November 1962, seven-year-old Olivia Dahl, never having been inoculated, came down with telltale symptoms —fever, coughing, and red rash. Within days, however, she developed a potentially deadly inflammation of the brain known as measles encephalitis and fell into a coma. On November 17, she died at seven years of age—the same age as Roald's sister Astri, who had died from acute appendicitis when he was only four. Dahl was still at the hospital with Olivia when the phone rang at Gypsy House. "Mrs. Dahl, Oliva's dead," a doctor told her mother, without emotion. "Did you hear me? I said Olivia's *dead*." Frozen with shock, she replied, "Yes, thank you" and hung up.

When Roald reached home, he was inconsolable. Pat stayed awake all night looking out the window, unable to believe what had happened. In the ensuing days, she recalled later, "Roald really almost went crazy. I held everything together. I cooked all day and went on. Of course 34 years ago anything like a survivors' support group was virtually unheard of. You had to pull yourself together. I loved Olivia, *loved* her, but . . . I had to go on." Roald too went on, of course. But he "couldn't say a word" over the years about Olivia, remembered Pat. "It was locked inside him," she said, for the rest of his life. He built a small memorial to her in the garden.

Believing that "a new child would begin to heal the emptiness," Pat hoped for more children. To her doctor in

California, soon after Olivia's death, she confided, "I absolutely believe in a soul. And I long to let her go, to free her and hope she will be born again to me." Two years later, she gave birth to Ophelia in 1964.

That year there were other signs that the Dahls were at last back on the road to the kind of lives they wished to lead. A year earlier in 1963, Pat had received an Academy Award for her role as Alma in the movie *Hud,* the story of Texas rancher violently at odds with his father. In 1964, Roald's rough draft of "Charlie's Chocolate Boy," originally begun in 1961, finally appeared in bookstores as *Charlie and the Chocolate Factory.* Then as 1965 began, Pat discovered she was pregnant again, a reason for further happiness.

One night in February, however, while Pat was giving the children a bath, she nearly fainted from a sudden pain in her head, and she became disoriented. At the hospital where she was taken by ambulance, doctors diagnosed a major stroke. Two more strokes followed, leaving her partially paralyzed, and unable to speak, read, or follow conversation. For anyone—especially for a mother of three children *and* an actress—her condition robbed her of almost everything except her life.

Once again, Roald valiantly struggled against adversity. He researched physical therapy and decided that the program the hospital offered Pat was inadequate. What she needed, he was convinced, was constant stimulus. Fearing she would lose her motivation if something wasn't done quickly, Roald called neighbors and friends to keep his wife busy every minute of the day, and Gypsy House became a kind of clinic. Many days, just as one friend would leave, having spent an hour in patient conversation with Pat, another one would arrive prepared to read

Pat and Paul Newman in **Hud.** *Pat earned an Academy Award for her role in the movie.*

her the newspaper. She was helped to walk and take care of herself, too.

The standard National Health Service program provided two half-hour sessions of therapy per week. Roald multiplied the amount by 30, and made sure his wife had six hours every day. For the next four years, he refined his methods into a step-by-step curriculum that became known as The Patricia Neal Therapy Extension Program, which is still in use at several stroke rehabilitation centers. In August 1965, just six months after her first stoke, she gave birth to Lucy, a healthy baby.

But for Dahl the writer, working steadily at his desk during those years was nearly impossible. In addition to running his wife's therapy, he insisted on running the household, too. He shopped, managed the finances, and took care of the family. Tessa recalled waking up one morning to see her name burned brown into the lawn. Roald had done it with weed-killer but claimed the fairies had been up to their tricks. He took his children out to eat and played their favorite game, which was choosing strangers and making up stories about them. Then Roald would call over the unwitting characters in his children's wild tales and ask them to introduce themselves.

Nevertheless, he did manage to get creative work done, too. He polished off a few short stories already begun before his wife's illness and wrote a several non-fiction pieces for magazines interested in how the family was coping. 1966 saw the publication of his children's book *The Magic Finger* about a pair of hunters who are shrink to the size of the birds they love to shoot. He also tried his hand at Hollywood scriptwriting. In 1967 he scripted the James Bond film *You Only Live Twice* based on a novel by his friend, Ian Fleming, and in 1968 he adapted Fleming's children's story *Chitty Chitty Bang Bang*. Also by 1968, Pat had recovered so well that she starred in *The Subject Was Roses* and received a nomination for an Academy Award.

The coming decade of the 1970s seemed promising. In fact, Roald was about to begin his most productive years yet as a writer.

Dahl adapted his friend Ian Fleming's book Chitty Chitty Bang Bang *for the screen.*

Roald and Pat at the Academy Awards in 1969. By this time Pat had recovered from the strokes and was well enough to have acted in **The Subject Was Roses,** *as well as receive an Academy Award nomination for her performance in that movie.*

6

Touching the Young Heart

"Dahl will lead a child out onto a windy limb and then suddenly he'll place a ladder underneath and the child will be able to get safely to the ground."

—Danny DeVito, producer, director
and co-star of "Matilda"

IT WAS AN accident how Roald Dahl became a children's writer during a period of his life when tragedy and triumph were coming in waves. The success of *Kiss, Kiss*, his 1960 collection of short stories for adults, left his publisher hungrily wanting more. But Dahl, a perfectionist when it came to his writing, had no ideas he thought were worth pursuing. Moreover, the demands of his wife's therapy made time for writing hard to come by. Rather than let his output come to a standstill, he turned to stories he knew well—the ones he'd been telling his children. "Had I not had children," he once remarked, "I would not have written books for children, nor would I have been capable of doing so."

Roald and Patricia had five children together–Olivia (who had died at age seven), Theo, Tessa, Ophelia and Lucy. Every evening, remembered Ophelia Dahl, "after my sister Lucy and I had gone to bed, my father would walk slowly up the stairs, his bones creaking louder than the staircase, to tell us a story. I can see him now, leaning against the wall of our bedroom with his hands in his pockets looking in to the distance, reaching into his imagination." And so it was the *James and the Giant Peach* was transformed from a bedtime story at Gypsy House into a book that appeared in the United States in 1961 and in Britain in 1967.

James is an orphan living with two cruel and physically abusive aunts. Magic seems to come to his rescue in the form of a bag of wonderful powder, but he spills it on the ground and a house-sized peach grows on a tree in his aunt's yard. He finds a hole bored into it and, crawling up inside, meets a band of talking insects who are ready for adventure. The peach rolls out of the yard, gruesomely crushing the aunts, and plops into the sea. Days later, largely due to James's courage and cleverness, the peach arrives in New York. By the end of the story, James is an independent, loved, and happy person—the way he was before his parents died.

The reviews of James's publication set the pattern for most of those written about Dahl's children's books—some

A scene from Willy Wonka and the Chocolate Factory, *the 1971 film adaptation of Dahl's 1964 book* Charlie and the Chocolate Factory. *Perhaps one of Dahl's best-known books, not least of all because of its subject matter, chocolate—something many kids the world over think about!*

praised his originality; others condemned the author's outlook. The reviewer for *The San Francisco Chronicle*, for example, called the book "the most original fantasy that has been published for a long time" and predicted that it "may well become a classic." *Kirkus Review* congratulated the author for "writing a broad fantasy with all the gruesome imagery of old-fashioned fairy tales and a good measure of their breathtaking delight."

The reviewer for *The Economist* magazine, however, faulted almost exactly what other reviewers found praiseworthy.

"Dahl's desire to be excruciating and so terribly odd and inventive seems actually to advocate murdering the more irritating members of the family and to make it sound acceptable." Respected children's book critic Ethel L. Heims wrote in *School Library Journal* that she strongly disliked Dahl's "violent exaggeration of language" and the "almost grotesque characterizations of the child's aunts."

Dahl shrugged off this and the criticism that later dogged his books. "Children know that the violence in my stories is only make-believe. It's much like the violence in the old fairy tales . . . These tales are pretty rough, but the violence is confined to a magical time and place. When violence is tied to fantasy and humor, children find it. . . . amusing."

In any case, proof of the book's popularity with children was plain enough. In 1962, its first year of publication, *James and the Giant Peach* sold 6,500 hardcover copies. By 1970, there were 115,000 copies in paperback and 45,000 in hardcover in the United Kingdom alone.

For his next children's book, Dahl relied for inspiration on one of his childhood loves—chocolate. Thinking back to the cravings of his sweet tooth when he was a teenager, Dahl remembered, "In the seven years of this glorious and golden decade (the 1930s), all the great classic chocolates were invented: the Crunchie, the Whole-Nut Bar, the Mars Bar, the Black Magic Assortment, Tiffin, Caramello, Aero, Malteser, Quality Street Assortment, Kit Kat, Rolo and Smarties. . . . I tell you, there has been nothing like it in the history of chocolate and there never will be." When he was a student at Repton Public School in Derbyshire, it had been his fantasy to visit the Cadbury Chocolate Factory not far away. In *Charlie and the Chocolate Factory*, which debuted in 1964, he lived out his dream.

Charlie Bucket lives in poverty eating boiled cabbage, but

Another scene from the 1971 movie Willy Wonka and the Chocolate Factory. Charlie and the Chocolate Factory, *like* James and the Giant Peach, *received both praise and criticism upon its release. Some found issue with the fact that the Oompa-Loompas were black pygmies from Africa, so Dahl made them white pygmies from "Loompa Land." They were changed for the film adaptation as well.*

he is obsessed with chocolate. Everyday on his way to school he passes a chocolate factory owned by an eccentric "candy man" named Willy Wonka. When Wonka holds a lottery involving five "golden tickets" wrapped inside Wonka bars, Charlie is overjoyed when he finds one. Not only do the winners receive a tour of the factory, but also a lifetime supply of chocolate. The other golden tickets end up in hands of Augustus Gloop, a fat boy who loves to eat;

Veruca Salt, a rich girl spoiled rotten by her parents; Violet Beauregard, who chews gum constantly; and Mike Teevee, who watches television all the time. Willy Wonka greets the winners at the gates and introduces everyone to his helpers, the 'Oompa-Loompas', described as pygmies imported from Africa.

But then, Dahl's trademark accidents to the wicked begin to happen, and each disaster is perversely funny. Augustus Gloop is sucked into a pipe on a chocolate riverbank; Violet Beauregard chews untested Wonka gum, turns blue and begins to blow up like a balloon; squirrels push Veruca Salt into a hole, thinking she is a bad nut; and in the television room, Mike TeeVee leaps into a television screen and comes out again only one inch tall. Wonka informs Charlie that he is the only one qualified to be the new owner of the chocolate factory.

Did you know...

Dahl's second book *Charlie and the Chocolate Factory* debuted first in the United States in 1964 and then in Britain three years later. Sales of the book climbed steadily internationally. The first printing of Chinese edition totaled two million copies. He wrote the screenplay for the 1971 film *Willy Wonka and The Chocolate Factory* starring Gene Wilder. Dahl was not a fan of the film after it premiered, but the movie continues to be popular on video. According to the Official Roald Dahl Web Site, a new version is in development.

A reviewer for *The Times* of London called it "the funniest children's book I have read in years; not just funny but shot through with a zany pathos which touches the young heart." The *Atlantic Monthly* described it as "full of magical nonsense and uproarious situations with a tiny germ of a moral artfully inserted in each chapter." The *New York Times Book Review* trumpeted that Dahl had "proved in *James and the Giant Peach* that he knew how to appeal to children. He has done it again, gloriously." Dahl was asked by the *New York Times* to pen an opinion piece on the state of children's literature. With characteristic bluntness, he pronounced that "five out of seven children's books published today are a cheat," written sloppily for a quick buck.

But Dahl's own creation was hardly faultless, either, according to some critics. Fellow children's author Eleanor Cameron objected to the book's "hypocrisy." On the one hand, she wrote, Dahl made it clear in the plot that he thought television-watching "is horrible and hateful and time-wasting and that children should read good books instead." On the other hand, she argued, the book itself wasn't much better than a Saturday morning cartoon show.

More serious complaints were yet to come. In 1970, dozens of schools banned *Charlie and the Chocolate Factory* because the African Oompa-Loompas worked like cheerful and mindless robots for white businessman Willy Wonka. Dahl apparently realized he'd opened himself to charges of racism. In the 1973 revised edition, the Oompa-Loompas are stout, wavy-haired white men who come from Loompa Land.

For her part, author Cameron still wasn't satisfied. In a series of articles for various journals, she stuck by her opinion that the book was phony, in poor taste, without literary merit, and only popular because to played to wish-fulfilling fantasies about candy that weren't very wholesome.

By the end of the 1960s, the emotional struggles connected with the death of his daughter and his wife's disabilities were largely behind him. The success of *James and the Giant Peach* and *Charlie and the Chocolate Factory* were proof that a second career as a writer—this time as a writer of children's literature—lay before him. And with the publication of *Fantastic Mr. Fox* in 1970, he began a string of best-selling children's titles.

Fantastic Mr. Fox involves a theme that interested Dahl—the relationship between animals and people. Mr. Fox steals chickens from three farmers to feed his family. The farmers hatch schemes to catch him, but each time Mr. Fox upsets their plans. Mr. Fox's clear conscience about stealing seems to suggest that Dahl believes creatures do what they must to survive or to take care of loved ones. The book was aimed at very young readers and did fairly well on bookstore shelves.

Dahl took a misstep however in 1972 with *Charlie and Great Glass Elevator*. His publisher had been pressing him for a sequel to the chocolate factory adventures, and Dahl reluctantly came up with a forced plot involving astronauts, aliens, and pills that act like the fountain of youth. The book turned out to be a mishmash of silliness and didn't receive glowing reviews.

But in *Danny, Champion of the World* (1975), Dahl returned to the path explored earlier in *Fantastic Mr. Fox*—people and animals, and stealing to survive. This time it's people doing the stealing. Danny's father is a poacher—someone who trespasses on people's property to hunt their wild game. When Danny learns the truth about his father, he is horrified at first. But his father convinces him that the rich people who own the land won't miss the game anyway, and

Danny is won over. The plot turns on the antagonism between rich and poor people. In addition, Danny comes to accept, as he says in the story, "that no father is perfect . . . grownups are complicated creatures, full of quirks and secrets . . . "

The book left open a number of ethical questions. One critic predicted that some readers would find the plot "unacceptable because the hero and his father are triumphant poachers; and if poaching can be presented as a heroic activity, what about shoplifting or any other kind of theft?" Other expressed bewilderment over whether Dahl was ridiculing the rich (when Dahl was rich himself) as land-owners or game-hunters, or both.

In *The BFG* (1982), Dahl fell back on his natural gift for merriment and fantasy. The Big Friendly Giant—referred to as the BFG—lives with ten other giants who regularly eat children. The BFG however would rather eat a vegetable called a snozzcumber, which earns him the contempt of the other giants. One night, as the BFG is skulking around a village trying to stay out of sight, an orphan named Sophie befriends him. Being different from most of their kind, they

Did you know...

Dahl once declared that "If you want to remember what it's like to live in a child's world, you've got to get down on your hands and knees and live like that for a week. You'll find you have to look up at all these . . . giants around you who are always telling you what to do and what not to do."

form a bond and hatch a plan to prevent the giants from eating any more children.

The BFG is a hilarious character who mispronounces words, belches, and "whizzpops." Dahl added bathroom humor, he said, because "Children regard bodily functions as being both mysterious and funny and that's why they often joke about these things. There is nothing that makes a child laugh more than an adult suddenly farting in a room." On the serious side, the story is about the weak outwitting the powerful, a favorite theme of Dahl's.

The Times Literary Supplement called *The BFG* "the funniest and most appealing book that Dahl has written for a long time," citing the book's "nonsensical wordplay and deliciously witty use of language." *The Spectator* enjoyed the "satisfyingly rude jokes."

And then, as if unable to resist flirting with controversy again, Dahl wrote *The Witches*, published only a year after *The BFG*. Some of Dahl's happiest summers as a boy were spent with relatives in Norway, which is where he sets *The Witches*. A seven-year-old boy is left in the care of his Norwegian grandmother after his parents are killed in a car accident. Unlike many of Dahl's other grown-up characters, the 86-year-old grandmother is a loving, responsible adult, despite being a little odd. For one thing, she is a witchophile, studying witches. They attend a convention for witches, where the boy overhears a plot to turn the children of England into mice. The witches punish him for eavesdropping and turn *him* into a mouse. To his surprise, he enjoys being a mouse. Then with his grandmother's help, he devises a plan to stop the witches' scheme.

Women belonging to witch societies wrote angrily to Dahl about his inaccuracies concerning witches. They especially resented the stereotypical portrait of witches as evil-doers.

The *Horn Book* magazine for teachers and librarians offered a lukewarm review. "Marred by a slow beginning and occasionally sexist statements," they wrote, "the book does not match *The BFG* in inventive word play or character; yet it is an appealing, fanciful tale of devotion." In 1990, the book was made into a film starring Anjelica Huston.

By the early 1980s, Dahl was in his mid-60s. His marriage to Patricia Neal came to an end in 1983 when they divorced after two years of separation. That year, he married Felicity Crossland, a family friend. In a thoughtful mood, Dahl next turned to himself as a subject to write about. Although he never wrote a complete autobiography, he provides sketches of his life in two short works of non-fiction: *Boy: Tales of Childhood*, published in 1984, and *Going Solo* in 1986.

Boy seems not to have been written to entertain children but almost as an explanation of why he empathizes with children. In many places, the book seethes with indignation over the way he was treated in school. A reviewer for *Horn Book* was probably right in thinking that "It is impossible not to wonder if the grim, almost Dickensian, school experiences have not been important in forging the dark humor and grotesque characters so often found in Dahl's books." *School Library Journal* was disappointed that because Dahl seemed unable to rid himself of anger over the injustices he had suffered, young readers of *Boy* missed out "what could have been a fascinating glimpse of the past."

In *Going Solo*, he struck a much happier note, perhaps because the time of his life covered by the book is when Dahl was finally on his own and independent. As a fighter pilot in World War II, he led an exciting and romantic (though highly dangerous) life. In fact, his cheerful tone contrasts so dramatically with the dreadful experiences he went though that the reader can't help coming away admiring him. A *Time* magazine reviewer summarized *Going Solo* as "a brief masterly remembrance of the gifts of youth and good luck."

Still, the injustices of his childhood seemed to torment him like unfinished business. In *Boy*, he had told the facts as he saw them about how cruel school authorities and adults can be. In *Matilda*, his next book, published in 1988, he let the art of fiction drive his points home.

Matilda is a genius in a family of fools. While she teaches herself to read and thirstily drinks in ideas at the library, her parents and brother watch television. They have nothing but contempt for her because her interests have nothing to do with material things they crave, like money, jewelry, clothes, and food. When she finally enrolls in school, she has to confront yet another pig-headed adult: the headmistress, Miss Trunchbull. Trunchbull is not only suspicious of

Did you know...

Until J. K. Rowling's Harry Potter books, *Matilda* broke all previous sales records for a work of children's fiction, selling half a million copies in six months after its publication. Rowling's *Harry Potter and The Goblet of Fire* broke all publishing records by selling 372,775 copies on its first day alone and went on to surpass Dahl's six-month record. However, in a 2000 poll taken in 4,000 bookshops and libraries in schools and on the web, Dahl was still voted Britain's favorite author by children and adults. Sales of his books total around 30 million.

anyone smart, but hates children to the point of physically abusing them. If Dahl hadn't exaggerated the awfulness of the school so much, the book might have been too grim. However, Matilda finds an ally in her teacher, Miss Honey, who appreciates Matilda's special powers. They become like mother and daughter, living together in fairytale happiness by the book's end.

The New York Times Book Review predicted that Matilda would, "surely go straight to children's hearts." The *Times Literary Supplement* praised Dahl for returning to his strongest themes, writing "Once again he has created a safe moral story in which children are given inventive powers . . . and revenge themselves humorously against their oppressors." *Matilda* was made into a film in 1996, directed by Danny Devito, who also starred in the film with his wife Rhea Perlman. Commenting on the Dahl's gifts as a children's writer, Devito said, he "will lead a child out onto a windy limb and then suddenly he'll place a ladder underneath and the child will be able to get safely to the ground."

The last book by Roald Dahl to be published during his lifetime was *Esio Trot* in 1988. Written for very young children, it tells a simple story of Mr. Hoppy and a widow, Mrs. Silver. She owns a tortoise, which she adores. Mr. Hoppy in turn adores Mrs. Silver and finds an ingenious way to win her love.

By then, Roald Dahl was an old man. He had spent almost 30 years sitting in the hut at the bottom of the garden of Gypsy House writing stories. What was it like in there, where he worked day in and day out?

Roald Dahl in 1971. His writing routine involved a particular kind of pencil, the same lunch everyday, and the absence of distractions such as telephones— all inside his workplace, a "hut" in the backyard.

7

The Hut in the Garden

*"You have to keep your bottom on the chair and stick it out.
Otherwise, if you start getting in the habit of walking away,
you'll never get it done."*

—Roald Dahl on the discipline of writing

FAMILY AND FRIENDS called the place where Roald Dahl wrote "the hut," but it was really styled after a gypsy wagon, or as the English call it, a caravan. Shortly after the Dahls moved to Gypsy House in Great Missenden in 1960, Roald had the caravan built. From the beginning, its purpose was to serve as his writing studio, never as a shed or playhouse—though it could have easily doubled as a playhouse with its curved roof, fanciful painted designs, and small steps leading up to a half-door entrance.

Inside, however, anyone could tell at a glance that it was someone's exclusive cubbyhole who made no attempt to keep the place tidy for anyone else. Covering the one window was a dirty plastic curtain. At the back of the caravan in the center of the room was a large leather wing-backed armchair that had belonged to Dahl's mother Mormor. On the wall behind the chair were drawings he liked, particularly by Quentin Blake, the best-known illustrator of his books. Dahl liked Blake and their relationship was highly productive. Most of the drawings weren't even framed but were simply pinned up.

On a table against the right-hand wall a bizarre collection of objects lay spread out. These had special meaning to Dahl, almost like charms. They included one of his hip bones that had been surgically replaced; a surprisingly heavy ball of silver paper from hundreds of chocolate bars he had eaten while at Repton Public School; a meteorite the size of a golf ball; a cone from cedar tree; his father's silver and tortoiseshell paper-knife; a model of a Hurricane fighter plane sent to him by a young reader; and a baby seal carved out of whalebone. Favorite rocks and minerals each had their own spots on the table, too.

But the caravan wasn't a memento museum. It was for writing, and when it came to writing, Dahl was disciplined. He was creature of habit—or maybe of ritual. The day began at 9:30 a.m. when he and a secretary would sort through the day's fan mail. Then around 10 o'clock, carrying a thermos of coffee, he'd head off to the hut. There was no phone out there, but when he was married to Patricia Neal, they devised a system so that if she needed him, she could push a doorbell near the back door of the house and it would flash the light in the caravan. One flash meant a visitor had arrived to see him; two flashes meant he was needed right away.

Sealed off by himself, he would first step into an old sleeping bag, which he drew up to his waist for warmth. Then he sat down on the chair, resting his feet on a suitcase filled with heavy logs that was tied to the chair legs so it was always at the perfect distance. Next came a thick piece of cardboard across his knees, and on top of that his green felt writing board.

He was extremely fussy about his writing materials. From a jar beside him, next to an electric pencil sharpener, he chose one of six pencils—there had to be six—always yellow Dixon Ticonderoga pencils, type 1388—2-5/10 (Medium). He had trouble getting them in England, and once became very put out when his publisher failed to send more from New

Did you know...

Dahl preferred to dress casually for work and play. His favorite combination was gray trousers, a striped shirt, and a cardigan sweater. But he was careful that his clothes were always of the best quality. His shirts were custom tailored in Scotland, and for sweaters he preferred the finest English wool or cashmere. But underneath? His first wife Patricia Neal said Dahl never wore underwear, revealing that "Underneath these outers he was always naked as a babe."

York. Finally, he was ready to get down to work.

He kept all his ideas in a red exercise book. If an idea came to him when the exercise book wasn't available, he would scribble on a piece of paper using anything—even a crayon or lipstick. He said it was important to jot down ideas, because "When I do get a good one, mind you, I quickly write it down so that I won't forget it because it disappears otherwise rather like a dream."

As a writer, he was a real plodder, sometimes spending six months on a short story and rarely less than a year on a children's book. *Matilda* stumped him. "I got it

Did you know...

Roald Dahl had many passions outside of writing. According to his widow Liccy Dahl, they ranged from "racing grey-hounds to breeding homing budgies [pigeons], medical inventions, orchids, onions, gambling, golf, wine, music, art, antiques and wine." What intrigued Dahl about orchids was the skill and patience required. "At first the excitement is simply in watching them flower, but then you start to breed them, crossing one with another, selecting the best and producing finer hybrids. Some people like tomatoes, I like orchids. Partly because of their beauty, partly because they are tricky to grow...it takes two years before any buds appear, and the flowers are very small. Several years must pass before the plants are mature."

Dahl and his wife Pat in 1970 on the set of the movie The Road Builder *which Dahl wrote for his wife. The film's plot involves a middle-aged woman who recovers from a stroke and a young mysterious man that she meets. Dahl also adapted* You Only Live Twice *and* Chitty Chitty Bang Bang *for the screen, which were books by his friend Ian Fleming.*

wrong. I spent 6 or 8 or 9 months writing it, and when I'd finished, it wasn't right. I mean it just wasn't right. I hadn't backed up and I hadn't kept changing, because the character, the main character the little girl keeps changing at you all the time and I hadn't bothered to go back and re-write for several chapters." So he started over from the beginning. He apparently never wrote a book without putting it through several drafts, and he relied heavily on his editors for advice.

He compared writing to going on a long walk "across valleys and mountains and things, and you get the first view of what you see and you write it down." Then he would continue on, letting his imagination ramble and getting different views of the story landscape. Finally, "The highest mountain on the walk is obviously the end of the book because it's got to be the best view of all" because, he said, it should be when the story all comes together as a whole—the big picture, in other words.

He said that he was fortunate because he laughed at the

Did you know...

At the top of Dahl's list of favorite books he wrote was *Danny, The Champion of the World*. Danny and his father live in an old gypsy caravan behind a filling-station, in the middle of the countryside. Danny admires his father, and is shocked to discover that his father is a poacher. In the dead of night, Danny's father sneaks into Hazell's Wood to poach pheasants from the tyrannical Victor Hazell. While Dahl was figuring out the setting of the story, he realized that his own property, and even his writing hut, provided the ideal location.

same jokes as children, and for any story of his to be worth its salt to children it had to be funny and fast-paced. In addition, the characters could not be ordinary, and he made sure they weren't by exaggerating their traits—"so if a person is nasty or bad or cruel, you make them very nasty, very bad, very cruel. If they are ugly, you make them extremely ugly. That I think is fun and makes an impact."

At noon he broke for lunch. He maintained that he could only write for a couple of hours, and after that he became "inefficient." Lunch was the same everyday: Norwegian prawns and half a head of lettuce. Then he would read or putter around the house or garden pursuing his hobbies until it was time to go back to the hut at 4:00 pm for another two-hour stint of writing.

His success as a children's writer came down to this, he said: he conspired with children against adults. "Parents and schoolteachers are the enemy," he said simply.

In 1990, Dahl was diagnosed with a rare blood disorder called myelodysplastic anaemia. In a newsletter to fans he wrote, "I've been a bit off-colour these last few months, feeling sleepy when I shouldn't have been and without that lovely old bubbly energy that drives one to write books . . . " He died on November 23, 1990 at the age of 74. At the time, he was working on *The Vicar of Nibbleswicke*, *My Year*, and *The Roald Dahl Cookbook*. His widow Felicity worked with his editors in getting the manuscripts ready for publication.

Roald Dahl in his later years. Though many critics would charge that his books were not always suitable for children, he would disagree and assert that he knew what children liked. Indeed, the enormous popularity of his books and movies adaptations from his books support his claims.

Giggles of Mirth

"I never get any protests from children. All you get are giggles of mirth and squirms of delight. I know what children like."

—Roald Dahl

WRITERS OF STORIES and novels are used to being asked, "Where do you get your ideas?" Roald Dahl's reply to this question was that "My ideas occur basically at my desk." By this he meant he started with the inspiration—say, a visit to a chocolate factory—and by trial and error expanded it into a story with characters, conflicts, and a plot.

83

But where did the inspirations for stories come from?

Nearly all writers of fiction rely at first on their own experiences. These can serve as the sources of serious or fanciful questions that the writer wants to explore. As a boy, for example, Dahl collected bird's eggs from their nests. In *Danny, Champion of the World* and *Fantastic Mr. Fox*, his characters defend poaching as their right. Or a writer's experiences can suggest situations that would be intriguing. Dahl went to Africa after high school. In *James and the Giant Peach*, James embarks on an incredible voyage to freedom and success.

Roald Dahl was no different from most fiction writers in this way. He tended to dip into his past for feelings and conflicts that were important to him. Even though he preferred fantasy for his children's stories—a world where a girl can befriend a lonely giant, for instance—a character's feelings of sadness, or anger, or excitement could still be genuine. He relied on his own feelings from childhood to make sure they were. But he was an exceptional writer, too—particularly because of his ability to express the viewpoint of a child or teenager in an entertaining story. And that has endeared him to millions of readers, besides earning the admiration of many critics.

However, there are others who question the appropriateness of his stories for children. They argue that his stories are bleak and bitterly funny, weighted too heavily with the author's personal bias toward life. In a piece about the movie *Matilda*, a reviewer for the *Sacramento Bee* wrote that "Dahl specialized in so-called children's books that were really books for adults who hated their childhood and held grudges against the adults who made life so miserable for them."

If Dahl's writings seem bitter at times, the origins of that attitude probably lie in his childhood and young adulthood, beginning with the sudden deaths in his family when he was four. His sister died, and then his father, perhaps from grief over his daughter's death. Roald may have believed he was cheated out of a father, who neglected him in a sense by wanting to be with his daughter more than he wanted to continue living to be with his son. If so, it would be understandable if he became convinced early on that life was unfair.

In his stories, he turns this brand of unfairness of being deprived of a parent into both a plot element and a theme. Children find themselves suddenly and unexplainably orphaned or rejected. James was happy in the beginning of *James and the Giant Peach* but then suddenly he is orphaned. His aunts not only reject him but also beat him and isolate him from everyone else. Matilda's parents treat her "as nothing more than a scab. A scab is something you have to put up with until the time comes when you can pick it off and flick it away." On issues like these, some critics argue Dahl goes too far. As one complained, "Child neglect countered by revenge, however funny and however justified, is just not a nice theme." Nice or not, Dahl could argue from first-hand experience that it happens.

A second childhood influence on Dahl's writing has to do with where he stood in English society. The Dahls were outsiders—Norwegian-speakers living in Wales, far from their relatives. Outsiders are as common in Dahl's stories as are orphans and rejected children. But they triumph, as Dahl tried to do again and again in his own life. Charlie Bucket is so poor he can afford only two chocolate bars in the hope of winning Willy Wonka's contest, but he does. Not only that, but by the book's end, he wins the entire chocolate factory. If Dahl did view himself as an outsider, perhaps that's why (as one critic points out) he preferred to work in his caravan, alone at the bottom of the garden away from his family. The isolation might have helped recreate old childhood feelings.

As Roald grew older, he attended boarding school. Judging from his experiences in *Boy*, he learned at school something else about unfairness—that it can be a tool of corrupt authority figures and bullies, allowing headmasters and older boys to beat the younger boys. In *Matilda*, the headmistress Miss Trunchbull grabs children by their ears and swings

Did you know...

"Roald Dahl hated museums but would have loved this," commented Felicity Dahl on seeing the Roald Dahl Children's Gallery in Aylesbury, England. The Gallery uses Dahl's stories to capture the imaginations of its visitors. Willy Wonka, the BFG and Fantastic Mr. Fox are part of interactive displays that encourage children to investigate history, natural history, science and technology. There are also large permanent displays, such as the Giant Peach, Fantastic Mr. Fox's tunnel, and the Twits' upside-down room. The Gallery, which is housed in an 18th-century coach house, has a capacity of only 85 people at a time, but a steady stream of museum-goers visits year-round.

them around, hurling them into the air, and everyone seems powerless to stop her. Just as bad as corrupt authority figures, in Dahl's opinion, are incompetent ones who permit cruelty. In *The BFG*, for instance, the Head of the Army and the Head of the Navy confess they can think of no way to stop the giants from eating children. Disgusted, the Queen calls them "rather dim-witted characters."

Some critics object to Dahl's tendency to divide the world into camps of victims and victimizers, powerful people and powerless ones, right and wrong. "The trouble with Dahl's world," wrote one, "is that it is black and white—two-dimensional and unreal." But once again, this was probably the way Dahl saw life— in terms of absolutes. If his son's brain injury could be helped with a better device, then Dahl helped invent it. If his wife could recover sooner with more therapy, then he turned most of her waking hours into one long therapy program. As his biographer Jeremy Treglown obeserved, in "Dahl's moral universe . . . there could be no question without an answer, no battle without victory."

Likewise, he deals with mean or cruel characters in his children's books the same way. In his story world, he said, "beastly people must be punished." Matilda targets Miss Trunchbull with her telepathic powers and terrifies the woman into running away. The Twits from the book *The Twits* use glue to catch unsuspecting birds, but instead come to a messy, gluey end themselves. Those who use physical violence get a good dose of it in return, too. The giants who eat children in *The BFG* are thrown into a pit for life, friendless, and left to beat each other up. Any young reader who's ever been bullied or harmed by someone more powerful would be tempted to cheer.

Dahl allows for an exception in his black-and-white world, however. Authority figures in loving families deserve obedience and trust. The grandmother in *The Witches* is an example, as is Danny's father in *Danny, Champion of the World*. There can be adult rescuers, too. Miss Honey in *Matilda* becomes a surrogate mother to Matilda and earns her love. The reason Dahl must allow that there are adults whom children can rely on is because his mother Sophie was one, and he showers praise upon her in *Boy*.

Dahl assures his readers who are struggling with issues of low self-esteem, loneliness, or the stress of unhappy situations that there is hope. Matilda, James, Danny, and Sophie are the reader's peers. They could even be the readers themselves. And because they are resourceful, self-directed, and persevering, they win in the end. An even more important message comes through in his books as well. "It doesn't matter who you are or what you look like," realizes the nameless boy in *The Witches*, "so long as somebody loves you."

Did you know...

In Great Missenden, where Dahl lived most of his life, plans are underway for the Roald Dahl Museum. In Cardiff, Wales where Dahl spent his childhood, the *South Wales Echo* newspaper is campaigning to have a street named after him.

Adults leveled criticism at Dahl's books from time to time, but he cared little whether he offended them or not. He wrote for children by sharing his feelings and experiences with them in stories. "I never get any protests from children," he said. "All you get are giggles of mirth and squirms of delight. I know what children like."

1911 Harald Dahl (Roald's father) marries Sofie Magdalene Hesselberg. They move to Llandaff, South Wales.

1916 Roald Dahl born in Llandaff, South Wales on September 13.

1920 Roald's sister Astri, 7, dies of an appendicitis. Months after his daughter dies, Roald's father Harald dies.

1923 Enters Llandaff Cathedral School.

1925 Enters St. Peter's School in Weston-Super-Mare.

1929 Enters Repton Public School in Derby.

1934 Graduates from Repton. Accepts position with Shell Oil company in London.

1938 Begins working at Shell's branch office in East Africa.

1939 Joins Royal Air Force. Learns to fly fighter planes in Nairobi, Kenya.

1940 Crashes in Libyan desert. Spends several months recovering in Alexandria, Egypt from serious injuries.

1941 Rejoins his squadron stationed in Greece.

1942 Begins working as an assistant air attaché at the British Embassy in Washington, D.C. His first published story, "Shot Down Over Libya," appears in the *Saturday Evening Post*.

1943 First book, *The Gremlins* is published under the name, "Flight Lieutenant Roald Dahl."

1945 *Over To You*, short story collection published. Moves to Amersham, England to be near his mother.

1948 First novel, *Some Time Never: A Fable For Supermen* published. Now divides his time between England and New York City.

1953 *Someone Like You*, a second short story collection published. Marries actress Patricia Neal on July 2.

1954 Roald Dahl and Patricia Neal purchase a farmhouse, Little Whittfield (later renamed Gypsy House) in Great Missenden, England. Wins Edgar Allan Poe award.

1955 Daughter Olivia Twenty born April 20.

1957 Daughter Chantal Sophia born April 11 (parents renamed her Tessa)

1959 Dahl wins second Edgar Allan Poe Award.

1960 Short story anthology, *Kiss Kiss* published. Son Theo Matthew Roald born July 30. Theo struck by a taxi in New York City and suffers massive head injuries.

1962 Dahl's first children's book, *James and the Giant Peach* published.
Daughter Olivia dies as a result of measles encephalitis November 17.

1964 Daughter Ophelia Magdalena born May 12. *Charlie and the Chocolate Factory* published.

1965 Patricia Neal suffers three massive strokes on February 17.
Daughter Lucy Neal born August 4.

1966 *The Magic Finger* published.

1967 Dahl screenwrites "You Only Live Twice."
Mother Sophia, dies November 17.

1970 *Fantastic Mr. Fox* published.

1971 *Willy Wonka and the Chocolate Factory* published.

1972 *Charlie and the Great Glass Elevator* published.

1975 *Danny, the Champion of the World* published.

1979 Adult novel, *My Uncle Oswald*, published.
Separates from Patricia Neal.

1982 *The BFG* is published.

1983 *The Witches* is published.
Divorces Patricia Neal on November 17.
Marries Felicity Crossland. Wins Whitbread Award.

1984 *Boy: Tales of Childhood* published.

1986 *Going Solo* published.

1988 *Matilda* published.

1990 *Esio Trot* published.
Dahl dies on November 23 in Oxford, England.

JAMES AND THE GIANT PEACH (1961)

CHARLIE AND THE CHOCOLATE FACTORY (1964)

THE WITCHES (1973)

DANNY: THE CHAMPION OF THE WORLD (1975)

THE TWITS (1980)

THE BFG (1982)

MATILDA (1988)

ESIO TROT (1990)

Novels and Short Non-fiction

THE GREMLINS (1943)

SOMETIME NEVER: A FABLE FOR SUPERMEN (1948)

JAMES AND THE GIANT PEACH (1961)

THE MAGIC FINGER (1966)

FANTASTIC MR. FOX (1970)

DANNY: THE CHAMPION OF THE WORLD (1975)

THE ENORMOUS CROCODILE (1976)

MY UNCLE OSWALD (1979)

THE TWITS (1980)

GEORGE'S MARVELOUS MEDICINE (1981)

THE BFG (1982)

THE WITCHES (1983)

DIRTY BEASTS (1984)

BOY: TALES OF CHILDHOOD (1984)

THE GIRAFFE AND THE PELLY AND ME (1985)

GOING SOLO (1986)

MATILDA (1988)

ESIO TROT (1990)

THE DAHL DIARY (1991)

THE MINPINS (1991)

THE VICAR OF NIBBLESWICKE (1991)

MY YEAR (1993)

Collections

SOMEONE LIKE YOU (1953)

KISS KISS (1960)

TWENTY-NINE KISSES FROM ROALD DAHL (1969)

SELECTED STORIES (1970)

SWITCH BITCH (1974)

THE WONDERFUL STORY OF HENRY SUGAR AND SIX MORE (1977)

THE COMPLETE ADVENTURES OF CHARLIE AND WILLY WONKA (1978)

TALES OF THE UNEXPECTED (1979)

TASTE AND OTHER TALES (1979)

MORE TALES OF THE UNEXPECTED (1980)

A ROALD DAHL SELECTION: NINE SHORT STORIES (1980)

ROALD DAHL'S COMPLETELY UNEXPECTED TALES (1986)

TWO FABLES (1986)

THE ROALD DAHL OMNIBUS (1987)

A SECOND ROALD DAHL SELECTION: EIGHT SHORT STORIES (1987)

AH, SWEET MYSTERY OF LIFE (1988)

THE BEST OF ROALD DAHL (1990)

THE COLLECTED SHORT STORIES OF ROALD DAHL (1991)

ROALD DAHL'S REVOLTING RHYMES (1995)

THE ROALD DAHL TREASURY (1997)

THE TWITS. Mr. and Mrs. Twit are an obnoxious couple who spend their lives trying to outdo each other in nastiness. But the Muggle-Wump monkeys and the Roly-Poly bird hatch an ingenious plan to deal them the ghastly surprise they deserve.

WILLY WONKA. Willy Wonka is the best of all chocolate-makers. He works in complete secrecy, however, a factory where no one ever goes in and no one ever comes out. When he offers a once-in-a-lifetime chance for five lucky winners to tour his factory, the result astonishes not only the winners, but the famous candyman, too.

JAMES. Orphaned by the sudden death of his parents, James is forced to live with two cruel aunts who isolate him from the world. But then a magical accident creates a giant peach. James crawls inside, finds new friends, and together they roll across the countryside, beginning a fantasy adventure. Facing all sorts of dangers, James finds that he is more resourceful and more courageous than he ever would have imagined.

MATILDA. Matilda is the neglected child of the tacky, gruesomely self-absorbed Harry and Zinnia Wormwood. Without any urging from them, Matilda teaches herself to read. Resentfully, the Wormwoods send their brainy daughter to school where yet another demented adult, Agatha Trunchbull, tries to squash Matilda's love of learning. Matilda finds a champion in her classroom teacher, Miss Honey. Encouraged by Miss Honey's affection, Matilda launches a counterattack on the adults ruining her life.

THE BFG. The BFG (Big Friendly Giant), unlike all other giants, is not fierce or brutish. However, he is rather slow-witted like others of his type. Nevertheless, he is determined to improve himself and has been reading "Darles Chickens" for 100 years. The BFG is an endearing character who doesn't mean to be funny, but he usually is.

Dahl received three Edgar Allan Poe Awards for his adult fiction from the Mystery Writers of America (1954, 1959, 1980). In 1982, *The BFG* won Federation of Children's Book Groups Award. In 1983, *The Witches* received the New York Times Outstanding Book Award, and the Federation of Children's Book Groups Award, and Whitbread Award. Dahl also received World Fantasy Convention Lifetime Achievement Award that year. *Matilda* won Federation of Children's Book Groups Award in 1988. *Esio Trot* won the Smarties Award in 1990. *Matilda* was voted "Nation's Favorite Children's Book" in British Broadcasting System

"An Interview with Director Danny DeVito." TriStar Pictures. 1996. *[www.spe.sony.com/movies/matilda/nickexclusive.html]*

"An Interview with Roald Dahl." The Roald Dahl Foundation. No date. *[www.roalddahl.org/index2.htm]*

Baltake, Joe. "'Maltilda' a Brave Film about a Child's Worst Terrors: Adults." Sacramento Bee. August 2, 1996. Posted by MovieClub. *[www.movieclub.com/reviews/archives/96matilda/matilda.html]*

Costell, E.O. The Warner Brothers Cartoon Companion. ("Gremlins") 1998. *[www.spumco.com/magazine/eowbcc/eowbcc-g.html]*

Dahl, Roald. *Boy: Tales of Childhood*. New York, Penguin: 1984.

Dahl, Roald. Danny, *Champion of the World*. New York, Puffin: 1998.

Dahl, Roald. *Going Solo*. New York, Farrar Straus Giroux: 1986.

Dahl, Roald. *James and the Giant Peach*. (reprint) New York: Puffin Books, 1988.

Dahl, Roald. *The Gremlins*. Completed text posted at Roald Dahl Fans.com. 2001. *[www.roalddahlfans.com/books/gremtext.php]*

Dahl, Roald. *My Year*. Viking, New York: 1994.

Dahl, Roald. "Shot Down Over Libya." The Saturday Evening Post. August 1, 1942. Reprinted at Roald Dahl Fans. Com. 2001. *[www.roalddahlfans.com/shortstories/shottext.htm]*

Dahl, Tessa. "Once Upon a Time, Childhood was Made of Magic . . . " The Sunday Times. April 23, 2000. Reprinted at Roald Dahl Fans.com. 2001. *[www.roalddahlfans.com/articles/once.php]*

"Dealing With Olivia's Death." People magazine. March 31, 1997. Reprinted at Roald Dahl Fans.com. 2001. *[www.roalddahlfans.com/articles/deal.php]*

"Epic Tale of Heroes Who Refused to Die." (G. Murray Levick and the Scott Expedition). The Daily Express. April 28, 2000. *[www.lineone.net/express/00/04/28/features/f0200scott-d.html]*

Erskine, David. "Roald Dahl and the Children's Gallery." British Interactive Group. Spring, 1998 (newsletter). *[www.big.uk.com/newsletter/98_spr/dahl1.htm]*

Farrell, Barry. *Pat and Roald*. Random House, New York: 1969.

Honan, William H. "Roald Dahl, Writer, 74, Is Dead; Best Sellers Enchanted Children." (obituary) November 24, 1990. The New York Times. Reprinted at Roald Dahl Fans.com. 2001. *[www.roalddahlfans.com/articles/obit.php]*

Howard, Kristine. "Controversy About 'Shot Down Over Libya." Roald Dahl Fans.com. 2001. *[www.roalddahlfans.com/shortstories/shot.php]*

Howard, Kristine. "My Dahl Biography." Roald Dahl Fans.com. 2001. *[www.roalddahlfans.com/mydahlbio.php]*

"ID Card: Roald Dahl." Penguin Books. 2001. *[www.puffin.co.uk/Author/AuthorPage/1,1590,000486,00.html]*

Liles, Caryn. "Boy Going Solo." (unpublished paper) April, 1999. Roald Dahl Fans.com. 2001. *[www.roalddahlfans.com/articles/boyg.php]*

Neal, Patricia with Richard DeNeut. *As I Am*. Simon & Schuster, New York: 1988.

Quick, Kevin. "Great Missenden." UK and Irish Genealogy. November 25, 2001. *[http://met.open.ac.uk/genuki/big/eng/BKM/GreatMissenden/Index.html]*

"Roald Dahl." (autobiographical statement) Educational Paperback Association. No date. *[www.edupaperback.org/authorbios/Dahl_Roald.html]*

"Roald Dahl." Books and Writers. 2000. *[www.kirjasto.sci.fi/rdahl.htm]*

Roald Dahl Biography. "The World's Favourite Children's Author." The Roald Dahl Foundation. No date. *[www.roalddahl.org/index2.htm]*

"Roald Dahl Voted the Country's Favourite Author." Whitaker BookTrack.World Book Day 2000. *[www.booktrack.co.uk/wbdwinner.htm]*

Round, Julia. "Roald Dahl and the Creative Process: Writing from Experience." (unpublished paper) Reprinted at Roald Dahl Fans.com. 2001. *[www.roalddahlfans.com/articles/crea.php]*

Royer, Sharon E. "Roald Dahl and Sociology 101. The ALAN Review. Fall, 1998. Vol. 26, Number 1. *[http://scholar.lib.vt.edu/ejournals/ALAN/fall98/royer.html]*

Schmid, Johannes. "Roald Dahl." Updated April 7, 1997. *[http://home.rotfl.org/me/r_dahl/r_dahl.html]*

Silver, Steven H. The Roald Dahl Treasury. (a review) SF Site. 1997. *[www.sfsite.com/12b/dahl23.htm]*

Soyka, David. The BFG (a review). SF Site. 1998.
[www.sfsite.com/10a/bfg42.htm]

Treglown, Jeremy. *Roald Dahl: A Biography*. Farrar, Straus, Giroux, New York: 1994.

Wright, Rebecca. "Roald Dahl: His Life and Literature." The Roald Dahl Chocolate Factory. 2001.
[www.geocities.com/Hollywood/Academy/4613/dahl.html]

WEBSITES

www.roalddahlfans.com/index.php
[Roald Dahl Fans.com]

www.roalddahl.org/index2.htm
[The Official Roald Dahl Web Site]

www.geocities.com/Hollywood/Academy/4613/
[The Roald Dahl Chocolate Factory]

www.buckscc.gov.uk/museum/dahl/index.stm
[The Roald Dahl Children's Gallery]

CHARLES J. SHIELDS writes from his home near Chicago, Illinois, where he lives with his wife, Guadalupe, an elementary school principal. Shields was chairman of the English Department at Homewood-Flossmoor High School in Flossmoor, Illinois. This is his fourth book for Chelsea House.